Nutkins on PETS

Written by
Terry Nutkins and Marshall Corwin

Illustrated by
Angelika Elsebach, Derek Matthews and Keith Field

Designed by
Charlotte Crace

Edited by
Lisa Hyde

CONTENTS

BBC

Introduction

When I was a boy we always had lots of pets in our house: dogs, frogs and all sorts of stray animals that I would bring home to look after. I lived in London, very close to London Zoo, and I first visited the Zoo when I was eight years old. After that first visit I could not take my mind off the elephants. I loved everything about them. They were so huge and yet so incredibly gentle. By the time I was ten years old I was helping the keepers to muck them out and give them their daily meal. I was amazed at how much each elephant ate and drank every day: a staggering 40 kg (90 lb) of hay, 10 kg (20 lb) of cabbage,

10 kg (20 lb) of horse nuts, 4 kg (9 lb) of carrots, 12 oranges, 12 apples, 6 onions, 6 potatoes and 200 litres (45 gallons) of water!

African elephants – my favourite animals.

Needless to say, it would be rather difficult and expensive to keep an elephant at home, but there are of course plenty of animals you can have as pets. Any animal is a great responsibility whatever its size – it is a living creature which depends completely on you to keep it alive and well and happy. But once you have decided on which pet you are going to keep and you understand the possible problems, it will be great fun and very rewarding. I hope that this book will tell you the main things you need to know.

Dolphins and killer whales have also been special friends of mine since I was a boy.

For each type of animal you'll find:

▶ an introduction to the pet, with advantages and disadvantages of keeping it, plus notes on its home and handling.

▶ a 'What do I need?' page: the pet's own guide to its needs!

▶ a Fascinating Facts File, including facts about some of the pet's wild relatives, marked with this paw sign 🐾

▶ a Pets' Problem Page, where I answer some of the most common questions about the pet.

TOP TEN TIPS

1 DO check in this book before you get a pet to make sure you have both the time and the money to look after it properly. Will you still care for it as much a year from now?

2 DON'T get a pet unless someone will be able to look after it when you are on holiday.

3 DO always be gentle and calm and try to be confident when handling pets. Animals can tell if you're nervous and then they get nervous too!

4 DO check how big the pet is going to grow. Will you be able to afford to house it and feed it when it's fully grown?

5 DO wash your hands before and after handling your pet. This will help stop your pet – and you – passing on germs.

PSSST! ~ ANNA BUYA GERBIL?

6 DO always buy pets from a reliable dealer. If possible, have the animal examined by a vet before you pay for it.

7 DO always put cages well away from draughts. Check in this book whether the cage or tank should be allowed to get any sun.

8 DON'T buy only one animal if it usually lives in a group. Will you be able to cope if the animals breed? If not, buy animals of the same sex.

9 DON'T touch wild animals (including birds) whether dead or alive, and never release your pets into the wild.

10 DO seek help from a vet as soon as possible if your pet appears unwell and you don't know what's wrong.

Dogs are the nation's number one animal with around seven million kept as pets. I have always had golden labradors myself, and over the years I've shared many adventures with them – one in particular lived to the grand old age of seventeen.

Deciding to get a dog is a very big step to take and should never be taken just because a puppy looks cuddly. Do you know how big it will grow? Will you be able to give it enough exercise? Who will look after it during the day? Can you afford the food? And what about the vet's fees?

I would recommend a small to middle size dog like a retriever or spaniel for the average family. Always choose a really lively puppy and if at all possible have it checked out by a vet before the sale is completed.

Kennel
A kennel in a completely enclosed garden is an ideal arrangement if you have to leave your dog alone for several hours each day.

Handling and training
It is essential to train your puppy. I have always believed that an obedient dog is a contented animal. Simple commands like 'sit', 'stay' and 'come' can be taught from the age of three months or so. The basic idea is to concentrate on one word at a time and repeat it over many fairly short training sessions. Have fun and give the puppy lots of praise and rewards even if, for example, you've had to push its rear end down into the sitting position to make it 'sit'!

Indoor bedding
Provide a basket or foam bed away from draughts and noise where the dog can lie down without being disturbed. Clean cushions and blankets regularly to get rid of fleas.

Bear in mind that a playful puppy will chew anything remotely chewable (including a foam bed), and will completely unravel a wicker basket.

A collar and name disc You're breaking the law unless I have your name and address on me when I'm out. My collar needs to be loose enough to slip a couple of fingers through. Don't spend a fortune on a collar when I'm a puppy – I'll probably grow out of it!

Exercise This should be regular – which means every day please! I like several romps in the garden, and although this may be enough for puppies and very small dogs, a dog as big as me really needs a long walk in the park as well.

What do I need?

A bone There's nothing quite like gnawing away for hours at a good large bone, but chicken bones and all cooked bones can splinter and really upset my stomach. Dog chews are safer and just as much fun.

Plenty of fresh water . . . should always be available, please. Milk is not necessary after I'm about six months old.

Vaccinations and worming As a puppy I'll need two sets of injections and some worm tablets when I'm a couple of months old, and then regular booster injections each year. It is very important not to let me out in the street or near other dogs until I've had my first injections.

Food Tinned foods are great, so long as you vary them a bit. Unless it says they are a 'complete meal' I'll need some dog biscuits as well. As a very rough guide a medium-sized dog like me needs a large tin of dog-food in the evening, with maybe some extra dog biscuits in the morning. Smaller dogs may like two smaller meals a day, and young puppies need to be fed even more often.

Little and large
Pet dogs vary enormously in size. This great dane, shown here with its puppies, weighs about the same as an adult human (70 kg). One of the smallest dogs is a chihuahua, which weighs only about as much as a bag of sugar (1 kg).

Who's afraid of the big, bad wolf?

Wolves usually hunt in packs of up to twenty, and a pack may kill as many as 200 sheep in a single night. When a wolf howls the whole pack usually joins in, and although this spine-chilling sound is often used to terrify people in horror stories, wolves will rarely attack a human except in self-defence.

The cunning fox

The fox has a reputation for working out clever ways to outwit farmers and kill their chickens. But it also does some good on farms by killing rabbits, hares and smaller rodents like mice. The red fox will eat just about anything, from deer to worms to scraps stolen from dustbins, although it will often hide away its less favourite foods until it is really hungry.

The dingo

This animal is a very close relative of the domestic dog which has lived wild in Australia for thousands of years. However, Aborigines train packs of dingoes to sleep next to them for warmth on particularly cold nights.

Haven't I smelled you somewhere before?

Dogs recognise each other by smell, often sniffing at each other's scent glands (situated under the tail near the dog's bottom). Like their wild relatives they mark out their territory as they walk along by urinating on obvious landmarks every few minutes.

Dear Terry

Q My friend's alsatian was shot dead by a farmer. Surely he's not allowed to do this?

A Well obviously I don't know the facts of this case, but in general farmers can do this if a dog is 'worrying' their sheep or cattle. I have to say that much as I love dogs I'm on the side of the farmer in this. They lose thousands of sheep each year, usually because pregnant sheep are so frightened by dogs that their lambs are stillborn. So whenever you are anywhere near sheep or cattle, keep your dog on a lead.

Q Do dogs hate travelling in cars?

A Not at all! Most dogs like it, so long as they've been taken out for a couple of ten-minute trips each day as puppies. Don't let them stick their heads out of the window though, and don't leave them for long periods in a parked car – many dogs die of heatstroke each year.

Q Our collie seems to be getting rather fat, even though she has a long walk every day. Should we put her on some sort of diet?

A Definitely. Give her even more exercise and cut down on food, especially dog biscuits. Try giving her green vegetables instead. Check on how she's doing by weighing her on the bathroom scales (hold her in your arms and see how much you both weigh, and then take away your own weight).

Q My parents say my dog should be neutered, but isn't this cruel?

A Not really, especially when you think of how many unwanted puppies there are already in the world. Neutering means a quick operation to make sure your dog can't breed: in a female dog it's called spaying and in a male dog castration.

Q Do all dogs scratch a lot? Our puppy seems to be scratching himself all the time.

A A lot of dogs do scratch a lot, but only because a lot of dogs have fleas (or possibly lice). You should immediately begin treating your puppy with powder or as recommended by your vet, but just as important you must also get rid of fleas and their eggs from the puppy's bedding (all of this is a very good reason not to allow your dogs on furniture or beds).

Q How do you 'house-train' a puppy?

A 'House-training' means training a puppy not to go to the toilet all over your house! Take the puppy outside for a few minutes every time you think it might want to do something, especially after a meal and when it wakes up. Reward it with lots of praise or a small treat when things go well, and scold it if it makes a mess inside – but only if the puppy's just done it, otherwise it won't know what you are on about and will simply get confused. Have patience: it takes a bit of time and the puppy's only doing what comes naturally!

Gerbils and hamsters

These delightful, friendly little creatures are among the easiest and cheapest pets to keep. They are great fun to watch, especially when making burrows or filling their pouches with food.

Gerbils and hamsters like very similar conditions, except that gerbils love company and hamsters prefer to live on their own. Also, hamsters need rather more cleaning out, and they sleep more during the day. (It's usually the early evening before they start to become very active, and if you're a light sleeper – beware! They can be scrabbling about all night.)

Tank

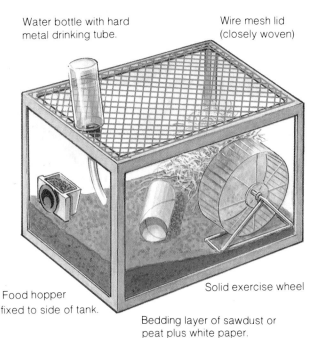

Water bottle with hard metal drinking tube.

Wire mesh lid (closely woven)

Food hopper fixed to side of tank.

Solid exercise wheel

Bedding layer of sawdust or peat plus white paper.

To allow gerbils to burrow fill the tank to about half way up (15 cm/6 in) with deep moss-peat and potting compost mixed with shredded white paper or straw. Keep damp and the burrows won't collapse.

Hamsters and gerbils are often kept in cages, though I personally feel that a tank with deep bedding is more satisfactory, as there is less likelihood of any draughts and it's closer to natural conditions.

Handling

To pick up a gerbil hold the tail *very* close to its body to keep it still, and 'scoop up' the animal with your other hand. Then cup it in both hands. Remember to be calm and gentle but confident too.

(To pick up a hamster do the same, but as shown hold the loose skin behind the neck instead of the tail. Never try to pick up a hamster when it's sleeping, as it may bite you.)

When you first get your animal don't try to pick it up for a few days. Stroke it gently and let it smell your hands until it gets used to you.

Hamster – Hold skin here.

Gerbil – Hold tail here.

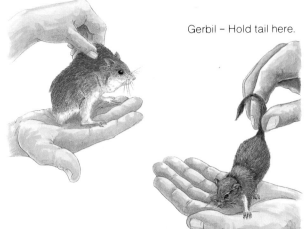

What do I need?

Water Hamsters can manage to go without water for a long time as we come from the desert, but please change it every day all the same. (Would *you* like to drink three-day-old water?)

A nice warm room . . . kept at about the temperature a human would like. Don't let my tank get direct sunlight.

Food I like a tablespoon of 'hamster mix' every day. For a treat please give me some green stuff or fruit once or twice a week.

No company I like to live alone. (Gerbils do like to live with friends, but only if they've known each other since they were very young – otherwise they fight.)

A good big home A large fish tank with a wire lid will suit me fine.

Cleaning out . . . every week or so. Let your nose be your guide! (Too much cleaning can be as bad as too little.) Scrub the tank with hot water and a little salt or special mild disinfectant. Rinse thoroughly. Please remove my droppings and any rotten food every day. (Gerbils will probably need cleaning out only about every two or three weeks.)

Lots to do I get bored otherwise! I can tear up white paper to make a bed, and I like to chew hard things like apple tree twigs to keep on wearing down my teeth. A solid exercise wheel is good fun, but please avoid cheap metal wheels with thin bars as I can hurt my paws on them or damage my nose gnawing them.

The grown-ups, age 45 days!
A baby hamster is born only about 15 days after the parents have mated (it's 9 months, of course, before a human baby is born). Just 45 days later the hamster has grown up and is ready to start having children itself.

Life is short

Hamsters do well to celebrate their second birthday, and gerbils are lucky to get to three. In fact, the heart of a gerbil or hamster beats about as many times during its lifetime as a human heart does, but because the little heart beats very much faster than a human's, life is very much shorter.

Saving for a rainy day

Many rodents store huge amounts of food in their burrows to help them through the winter. In one gerbil's burrow over 50 kg (8 st) of food was found. That's like the weight of fifty bags of sugar. (Rodents also store a lot of food in their cheeks when they're eating, so don't worry if their faces look really swollen.)

Marathon runners

Hamsters are mainly nocturnal: they sleep in the day and come out at night. They are thought to cover about 8 km (5 miles) a night looking for food (so make sure you provide an exercise wheel!).

Busy as a beaver

The beaver is the champion rodent for sharp teeth. It's been known to gnaw through a tree trunk one metre thick in a single night.

Non-stop teeth

Gerbils and hamsters are rodents, which means their teeth never stop growing. Rodents have to gnaw on something hard like wood or dog biscuits to keep their teeth filed down. If they can't find anything hard to chew on, the teeth can grow right round their jaws and fasten their mouth shut.

Dear Terry

Q My mother has a cold. Can she pass it on to my hamster?

A Definitely, and to other rodents too, so if anyone has a cold or sore throat don't let them handle or come near your pets as these illnesses are more serious in such small animals.

Q I've a hamster and he seems to have a sort of wet tail all the time. Is this normal?

A No, though it is very common. Your hamster has a sort of diarrhoea which is indeed known as 'wet tail'. It's thought to be caused by the hamster's eating habits and it's often hard to cure. Sometimes less fat in the diet with extra vitamins helps, but ask your vet's advice. (Never allow your hamster or gerbils to play on the carpet, by the way, because they'll be tempted to eat bits of it and will almost certainly end up with diarrhoea. They might even gnaw an electric cable and end up dead.)

Q I think my hamster may have a skin disease with two patches of dark hair on each side near the back.

A Many owners are fooled by this! These patches – which are more obvious in males than females – are perfectly normal and are the sites of special glands. However, if you notice skin problems like bald patches see a vet. Skin diseases include ringworm (caused by fungus) or mange (caused by mites), but may just be due to old age.

Q My gerbils look like they have sore noses. Do they have a cold?

A Possibly, but it's far more likely that the gerbils have been hurting their noses by chewing at metal bars. This is one of the reasons I recommend that you keep them in a glass tank and provide something hard like twigs to gnaw on.

Q I'm very worried because my gerbil keeps having a sort of fit, where it bunches up and shivers with its fur bristling.

A Yes, this always looks alarming, but rest assured that it's quite common and the gerbil doesn't seem to suffer any long-term harm from these seizures. They are often brought on by too much handling or by a sudden shock, and you should put the animal back in the tank with its fellow gerbils straight away and leave it undisturbed.

Q I thought my hamster was dead but later in the day it was all right. Can you tell me what happened?

A Well, to my knowledge hamsters don't have more than one life, so it almost certainly went into temporary hibernation. It probably suffered a sudden drop in temperature (was there an unusually cold night?). If you are ever unsure whether your hamster or gerbil really is dead, cup it in warm hands and see if it recovers.

Birds

There are many sorts of bird which are bred in captivity and can be kept as pets, though larger exotic birds like this beautiful cockatoo are quite a handful and can be very expensive. The most popular pet bird in Britain is the budgerigar: it is thought that we keep somewhere between two and six million of these attractive, undemanding pets. They are reasonably cheap, very colourful, and if trained early enough will even talk to you. On average they live for seven or eight years.

Cage

Toys (but do not clutter up the cage)

High perch (fruit tree branch preferred)

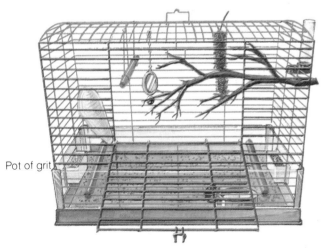

Pot of grit

Sand or sandpaper

Lower perches near food and water containers

Aviary

An aviary needs both an outdoor area and an enclosed area, and should be south-facing to get warmth from the sun. It's advisable to build it on concrete, as rats can gnaw through a wooden floor.

Handling

Birds generally do not like to be handled. No matter how careful you are, feathers usually get ruffled. However, you can often train them to perch on your finger. If you must handle a bird put your hand over it as shown and hold its head gently between your first two fingers. To catch a bird in an aviary you'll probably need a net.

What do I need?

Grit I know it sounds strange but I swallow it to help me digest my food.

Home . . . is either a large cage indoors or an aviary outside. I much prefer the aviary because I like the feeling of freedom and I can fly about with lots of fellow budgies.

Water Although I may not drink often, please give me fresh water every day. I also like a bath every couple of days, so provide a saucer of luke-warm water for me to splash about in – preferably in the morning so I've got time to dry off before nightfall.

Food Mixed seed bought from the pet shop will do nicely, plus a little green salad or dandelion each day. As a treat I like a bit of apple or carrot.

Exercise In the wild my ancestors were used to flying huge distances across Australia, so I must get lots of exercise. If I'm kept in a cage, please let me out for as long as possible each day to enjoy some freedom and fly around the room. But keep doors and windows closed and chimneys blocked or I'll be off.

No smoking Smoke and kitchen smells bother me. Also, my cage needs to be kept out of draughts and away from direct sunlight. If you're going to keep the light on all evening, cover my cage with a dark cloth so I can get some sleep.

Cleaning out My cage should be cleaned out every couple of days, and lined with fresh sand or sandpaper. Clean out the seed container and the grit pot every week, otherwise dust collects in the bottom and that might mean mites.

Olympic champions
The sprint champion on the ground is the ostrich at 70 km/hr (45 mph).
The 'diving' champion (amongst birds of prey swooping for their victims) is the gyr falcon which has been timed at about 200 km/hr (125 mph).

Winter sun

Each autumn about 5000 million birds set off on the long journey to spend winter in the warmth of Africa. This is called migration and birds may cover thousands of miles in each direction. During migration young birds will find their way without any help from their parents.

The Arctic Tern migrates all the way from the north pole to the south pole, a round trip of about 25 000 miles each year. This makes it the greatest traveller in the whole of the animal kingdom.

The world's tiniest helicopter!

The hummingbird can hover in the air or even fly backwards, beating its tiny wings about 70 times a second. The bee hummingbird is the tiniest bird of all. At about 5½ cm (2¼ in) long, and weighing about 1½ g (1/20 oz), it's smaller than some insects and would just about fit inside a matchbox.

Why would a woodpecker peck?

The male woodpecker drums so hard with its beak on trees and telegraph poles that the sound can be heard well over a mile away. The drumming – ten to fifteen blows each second – is nothing to do with feeding but attracts females and warns off other males.

Violent vultures

Vultures feed mainly on the remains of dead animals. The bearded vulture gets impatient and pushes live animals over cliffs and off the sides of mountains so that it can feed on the dead bodies.

Dear Terry

Q I'm worried because my canary has stopped singing and seems to be losing his feathers.

A Fear not! It sounds like he is moulting. This always happens at the end of summer and the old feathers will soon be replaced with new ones. Try not to disturb him too much during this period, which lasts for a month or so. (Note, by the way, that female canaries never sing.)

Q I'm worried because my budgie's cere (the bare bit above his beak) has gone very blue and he keeps throwing up.

A Fear not either! This often happens when he is ready to breed and is quite normal. If he had a mate he would throw up his food so he could give it to her. Instead he may well be sick over one of his favourite toys! Female budgies (which have a brown cere) may also do this, but usually rather less.

Q My parents don't want me to let my budgie out of its cage because they say there will be droppings all over the living room. Is this true?

A There may well be droppings in the two or three places where the budgerigar likes to perch in the room. But tell your parents that the droppings are almost completely dry so they will do no damage – and also that you'll brush them up!

Q How can I train my bird to come back to its cage if I let it out for exercise?

A It's probably best to spend a few days training it to perch on your finger before letting it out into the room. Hold your forefinger near the bird in the cage. Talk gently to it and perhaps tempt it with some lettuce or dandelion. Each day move your hand further away from the open cage door till the bird is completely used to perching on your finger. Eventually it should be happy to hop back onto your forefinger wherever it is in the room. If you are having real trouble drop a duster or tea-towel over it to catch it, and then grasp it gently as shown in the 'handling' section.

Q One of my budgies has gone very quiet and is just sitting on its perch with its feathers all fluffed up. Is it ill?

A Yes, this is typical of a bird that's not well. You should keep it warm and have it seen by a vet as soon as possible. (Other common signs of illness are wheezing, and blood in the budgie's droppings.)

Q My friend has gone to live abroad and I have taken her pet cockatiel. It is about two years old and although it can whistle it can't talk at all. How long will it live, and how can I teach it to talk?

A First of all, congratulations on getting such a wonderful pet. As you may know, cockatiels are kept in very similar conditions to budgerigars, though their cages should be rather bigger. Outdoors, cockatiels and budgies can share the same aviary. On average they live about twice as long as budgies – fifteen years or so. As for talking, I'm afraid it's now unlikely. Birds of the parrot family usually need to be taught to speak before they are six months old. (It's done by repeating the same word over and over, often for days on end.)

Ponies and horses

Smells bring back some memories very clearly, and whenever I'm near a horse or a pony the smell of the animal reminds me of cold winter's mornings mucking out stables and grooming the animals for hours on end. Ponies are great company and can give a huge amount of pleasure, but they are also very expensive both to buy and to keep.

If you are thinking of getting a pony of your own I would recommend that you first of all help out at some local stables to see what is involved. When you have found a pony that you want to buy, ask a vet to give it a thorough examination and advise you on whether it's going to be a suitable breed for you. All these preparations will make sure that you and your pony have a very rewarding partnership – which could last for twenty years or more.

Stables

Permanent ventilation high up to avoid draughts

Separate room to keep tack

At grass

When keeping ponies out in a field ('at grass') allow an area about half the size of a football pitch for each pony. The field should be completely enclosed by a hedge or a wooden fence (note: no wire or sharp pointed posts). Make sure the gate has a secure catch.

Door wide enough to let pony through easily

Door is divided for ventilation and to let the pony look out

Two bolts on lower door

Pony's area at least 3 m × 3 m (10 ft × 10ft)

Handling and exercise

Ponies can be very easily frightened so you need to be especially calm, gentle and confident when you approach them. Talk quietly to them and don't surprise them by coming up from behind.

Learn to lead and ride a pony at your local stables. Exercise your own pony very gently at first, and remember that it is not a good idea to go round and round your field: the pony will get bored and you'll damage the grass.

Home . . . is either a stable or a large grassy field with a shelter for very cold nights. I prefer the freedom of living outside, but it's nice to know there's a stable I can stay in if I'm ill or if there's thick snow on the ground.

Water I like lots of fresh water every day, but don't give me much water straight after exercise otherwise I may get colic (bad stomach pains).

Cleaning out If I'm in stables you must 'muck out' early each morning, which means getting rid of all soiled bedding and then moving dry bedding to one side while you wash the floor. If I live in a field, please pick up my droppings each day.

What do I need?

Shoeing and worming My farrier (foot expert) should see me about every six weeks or so to change my horseshoes and look after my hooves. I also need worming regularly.

Grooming If I'm kept mainly in stables and ridden a lot my coat should be clipped. I like being brushed down every day to get rid of dirt and give my skin a massage. If I'm kept outside I'd rather you didn't clip or groom me – I need my coat to keep me warm and waterproof, and I'll roll over if I want to clean myself.

Food In the stable I'll need a lot of hay each day and some 'pony nuts' or 'pony cubes', especially if I'm being ridden a lot. I also like a few apples or carrots as a treat. If I live outside I'll need hay right through the autumn and winter because I can't eat the grass then.

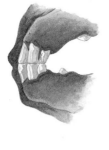

Never look a gift horse in the mouth

This old saying came about because the angle of a horse's front teeth helps tell you the age of the horse: the greater the angle, the older the horse.

The zebra's stripes

Nobody really knows exactly why zebras have stripes. Unlike the markings on many animals, the stripes are certainly not for camouflage – they don't help a zebra blend in with anything (except perhaps a zebra crossing!). Indeed, zebras never try to hide when enemies approach, preferring to stay in large groups in the open. One idea is that when a group of zebras are standing close together all the stripes dazzle the enemy and make it hard to judge how far away the animals are.
A zebra's stripes are like a fingerprint – no two zebras have exactly the same pattern.

A pony or a horse?

Ponies are not young horses: they are completely separate breeds. Although they are usually smaller than horses, this is not always the case. For instance, some Arab breeds of horse grow to only about 13 hands (130 cm or 4 ft 6 in), whereas the tallest polo ponies are about 16 hands (160 cm or 5 ft 4 in).

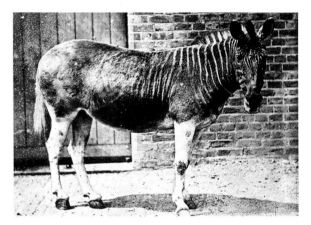

Zebras under threat

Several types of zebra are in danger of becoming extinct: they are hunted by humans for their beautiful skins. But it's already too late for the South African quagga, a rather special zebra which had stripes only on its head and neck. The quagga was completely wiped out just over a hundred years ago, and will never be seen again.

The horse's mane

The domestic horse is the only member of the horse family whose mane falls to one side. The manes of wild horses, asses and zebras all stand up like a brush.

Dear Terry

Q I've just begun jumping but my pony's got really difficult to control. He used to be so calm. What's happened?

A *Too many oats, I expect! If you're starting to give your pony a lot more exercise it is very important to give it extra food like pony nuts or crushed oats. But unfortunately too many oats can make a pony too lively.*

Q We bought our pony just over nine months ago, and I've noticed that she seems to have a large belly. It's a bit like she's pregnant, though she's not been near a male pony. What's the matter with her?

A *She is pregnant! It takes about eleven months before a foal is born, and often you don't notice that a mare (female pony) is pregnant till quite late on. So she was probably pregnant when you bought her. Have her seen by a vet immediately. You will need to change her diet, and you may want to make arrangements for*

someone else to look after the foal once it's born, because it's really a job for an experienced person.

Q Every time I leave my pony in his stable he seems to be able to open the door and get out. Is he a genius and would you like him to be on television?

A *Well, thanks for the offer but we would have an awful lot of ponies on TV, because just about every pony can figure out how to undo a simple latch. That's why it's important to have two good bolts on the stable door.*

Q I keep my pony out in a field and she's started walking funny and limping badly. I can't understand it because her shoes seem all right and I don't think there are any stones in her feet.

A *Ponies often have foot problems and this sounds like a particularly serious one called laminitis, so you should have your pony seen by a vet immediately. Laminitis is a very painful swelling of the feet which can make your pony permanently lame. It's usually caused by eating too much lush grass in the spring and you may find your pony has a lot of stomach pains as well. The only real answer is to keep ponies in stables when the grass is growing very fast around April or May.*

Q When I ride my pony he gets out of breath very quickly. Is there anything wrong with him?

A *It may be that you're trying to give him too much exercise too quickly. Remember that if you don't ride him all week you should only exercise him very gently at weekends. If he breathes very heavily almost immediately then I'm afraid it may be too late and he may have what's called 'broken wind', which is permanent lung damage caused by too much exercise when a pony's not fit.*

Snakes

Handling
Pick the snake up at the centre of its body or near the head. Allow the snake to move slowly through your hands giving plenty of support. Hold it over the tank otherwise you may lose it if it suddenly decides to move like lightning.

Just that word 'snake' sadly brings fear to many people, and children usually pick up the fear of snakes from their parents. In fact many of the 2400 types of snakes in the world aren't poisonous at all and make surprisingly good pets, although they do take a bit of looking after. I have friends who even keep pythons and boa constrictors, but big exotic snakes like these can be dangerous and must be handled with care. They also need a very large tank.

A charming little snake to start with is the garter snake which grows to about 1 m (3 ft) at most, and when young is only about the size of a pencil. It's completely harmless and indeed the main danger is that you'll accidentally harm the snake. But take good care of it and I guarantee you'll spend hours being amazed at how it slides along, how it sheds its skin, and how it gulps down food that looks too big to go in its mouth! Garter snakes live for up to twelve years.

Tank

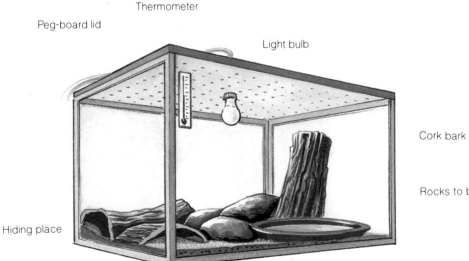

Thermometer

Peg-board lid

Light bulb

Cork bark

Rocks to bask on

Hiding place

Water dish big enough to take snake's entire body. Change water every couple of days.

With the arrangement shown, you'll need to keep switching the light bulb on and off to keep the temperature as near as possible to 25°C. If you can afford it, it's better to get a heater instead with a built-in thermostat (this switches the heater on and off automatically).

What do I need?

A long rest after eating   Please leave me alone for one or two days after feeding. Don't try to handle me or I may be sick.

A hot light . . . to sunbathe under where the temperature is around 25°C.

A wooden cage . . . for a home with somewhere to have a bath. (An old fish tank will do instead, though the metal bits may get a bit cold for me.)

Food   Don't be fooled by my small head. I can eat some pretty big stuff. Feed me about once a week on whole fish (such as whitebait or small sprats), earthworms, strips of meat or fish dipped in vitamin powder with calcium (these can be bought from good pet shops).

Cleaning out   Remove my waste droppings using old rubber gloves or with your hand in a plastic bag. Wash out the tank completely about once a month with warm water and a special mild disinfectant. Rinse thoroughly.

Danger – poison!

It's thought that at least 35 000 people die each year as a result of snake bites. The king cobra is one of the world's most dangerous snakes. It grows to over 5 m (17 ft) long and one bite with its highly poisonous fangs is enough to kill a large animal like an elephant. (The fangs are hollow and the poison is 'injected' down the middle of them.) The spitting cobra aims to blind its victim by squirting its poison at the eyes. It is usually deadly accurate up to 2 m (7 ft) away.

My next trick is impossible

The jaws of snakes 'unlock', allowing them to eat things bigger than their own head. Large pythons have been known to eat whole pigs and the African egg-eating snake swallows whole eggs about twice as wide as its body, shells and all. Special bones in the snake's throat then break up the egg and the shell is eventually spat out.

The fastest snake is the black mamba which wriggles at up to 20 km/hr (12 mph). It's a terrifying sight because it zooms along with its head up in the air, mouth open and tongue flicking out. The high jump champion is a type of viper which can leap over 1 m (3½ ft) in the air to bite its victim.

Snake music

The rattlesnake warns its enemies to stay away by shaking rapidly the 'rattle' at the end of its tail. The 'rattle' is made up of hard round sections which are loosely joined together, and the noise it makes is loud enough to be heard about 30 m (100 ft) away.

Supersense

The pit viper can track you down and bite you in complete darkness. Two holes (or pits) near to its eyes can 'see' the infra red rays given off by anything warm – including a human body.

Dear Terry

Q Have you any advice to cure my younger brother? He's really frightened of my snake. I keep telling him that it's not poisonous and can't hurt him, but he won't even come into the same room.

A It's very hard to stop people being frightened of certain animals, no matter how silly their fear seems to you. With a snake they're often afraid that it's going to crawl over them or bite them, and they think it's going to be 'all slimy and horrible'. Promise not to open the tank and see if your brother will come in and watch your snake. Later you may be able to persuade him to touch it either in the tank or while you hold it. He'll be pleasantly surprised to find that snakes are dry and scaly – not slimy at all! It's important to remind people who are scared of animals that the animal is probably far more frightened of them! So they must try to be gentle, calm and confident in front of the animal – even if that's not how they feel inside. If your brother really doesn't think he can do this, then you're just going to have to keep your brother and your snake in separate rooms.

Q I have kept garter snakes for a few years and I would like to get a python or even a poisonous snake. Can you give me any advice?

A In general my advice would be quite simple – don't! Pythons need very special care, including a very large tank and a constant supply of mice, rats and chicks for food. Many end up being given to zoos and safari parks because they become too much for their owners to look after. Poisonous snakes can obviously be very dangerous, and only people over eighteen with a special licence are allowed to keep them.

Q My snake seems to have small brown things crawling around in his skin. Should I do anything about them?

A Yes, they are mites and they can spread disease. Hang a 'Vapona' strip in the tank for a couple of days and this will kill the mites. Then repeat about a week later in case any new mites have hatched.

Q My garter snake doesn't seem very well. He's off his food and his skin doesn't look right – it's gone sort of greasy.

A This sounds like his tank has got too damp. Although a lot of garter snakes come originally from warm, damp places, they must have dry bark and rocks to rest on. Make sure that the pool area doesn't keep overflowing and wetting the rest of the tank. You should also take your snake to a vet – if he's not cured quickly his skin will break out in sores and he may die.

Q I have a garter snake and I'm worried because its eyes have gone all cloudy. Is it going blind?

A Yes, a little bit, but only for a few days. This is perfectly normal and as you've probably discovered by now it happens a couple of days before the snake sheds its skin. It's always fascinating to watch a snake wriggling out of its old skin (which is usually left behind in one piece, including the eye coverings). This takes place every three or four months and is called 'sloughing'. Generally, young snakes shed their skins more often than older snakes to allow them to grow.

Fish

Fish are not a pet to stroke and handle, nor will they show you a great deal of affection, but they can be quite beautiful and extremely relaxing to watch. The common goldfish is probably the most popular and the most suitable fish to start off with. It's not often realised that if kept out in a garden pond goldfish can grow up to 40 cm (16 in) long and live for 25 years. In a tank they may stop growing at about 10 cm (4 in).

Although some of the fancy breeds of goldfish may look more spectacular than the common goldfish, they will live only about half as long and may not be tough enough to live outside in a pond.

Tank

Tank at least 45 cm (1½ ft) long, 30 cm (1 ft) wide and 30 cm (1 ft) tall.

Change about one third of the water every two or three weeks, or sooner if it goes a bit cloudy. (Try to avoid changing all of the water if possible.) Top up using water which has stood in the same room overnight.

A lid (with holes for ventilation) will keep cats and dust out – and fish in!

Position the tank where it will not get direct sunlight. A heater is not necessary in the average room.

Using a bubbler and underground filter keeps the water clean. You can keep more fish too!

Clean, washed gravel. Put it in a sieve under the tap before you use it.

Pond

All but the most fancy breeds of goldfish will do extremely well in a garden pond. As long as the water is about 45 cm (18 in) deep and clear of dead leaves, the fish will survive the coldest winter – even if the pond gets iced over. But don't break the ice or the shock may kill them!

What do I need?

Food . . . a very small pinch of good quality fish food or pellets once a day. (If I haven't eaten it all in about ten minutes you've probably given me too much.) Treat me to green food like chopped lettuce and live food like daphnia two or three times a week.

A constant temperature   I'm 'cold-blooded' so I don't mind too much what the temperature of the water is (so long as it's between about 10°C and 20°C). However, I am very sensitive to sudden changes in temperature. Topping up my tank with water that's much warmer or colder may even kill me.

Home . . . is a nice big tank with interesting stones to swim through and hide behind. Include some plants and snails if you can, but please avoid any sharp objects as I may damage my scales.

Company . . . but please don't overcrowd the tank. As a very rough guide see how many of these books would fit over the surface of the water – that's how many of us can live and grow comfortably in the tank (with a good bubbler you'll be able to keep one or two more).

I hate goldfish bowls   Please *never* put me in one: they're too cramped and there's too little surface for the amount of water. (I need a large area of surface so that enough oxygen from the air will dissolve into the water.)

No shocks   Tapping on the side of the tank really upsets me, and if you have a light in the tank please don't turn it on and off when the room is dark. If you must transfer me to another tank use a large net – not your hands.

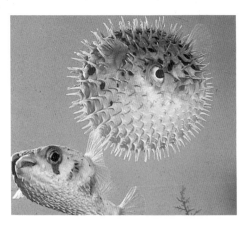

Fish out of water

Mudskippers and lungfish both spend long periods out of water, using their front fins like little legs to crawl along the ground. They are able to breathe by dissolving oxygen straight through their skin (though they have to keep it wet by rolling over in the mud). Lungfish in desert regions have been known to survive for several years when their ponds have dried up. They bury themselves in the mud and go into hibernation until the rains come.

Jaws

Sharks have immense powerful jaws which can easily bite through a thick steel cable. They also have a keen sense of smell which can pick up a trace of blood in the water about 200 m (220 yds) away. Nevertheless, several types of shark, including the huge whale shark, are not man-eaters at all. The whale shark is the biggest fish in the world growing up to 18 m (60 ft), about the length of two buses, but it feeds only on tiny shrimp-like creatures.

Fish or mammals?

Quite a few of the large creatures that swim in the sea are not fish at all. Whales, dolphins and seals are all mammals – like humans they breathe air and have to come to the surface from time to time to take a breath. But a champion diver like the sperm whale can hold its breath for up to an hour, diving to depths of more than a mile (1½ km).

Strange sight

Fish like plaice and sole have both eyes on the same side of their head. When they first hatch they have an eye on each side, but for camouflage they spend most of their time lying flat on their side in the sand at the bottom of the sea. So over a period of time one eye moves round to give it more chance of getting used – and less chance of getting sand in it!

Dear Terry

Q I've got a very big aquarium and I'd like to get some tropical fish to go with my goldfish. Is this a good idea?

A No. Tropical fish need a constant temperature of about 24°C (75°F), and you should be keeping your goldfish rather cooler, between 10°C and 20°C (50°F to 70°F). If you decide to go ahead you'll need to buy a separate tank and a heater. Remember also that tropical fish are usually much more expensive than goldfish.

Q Why do goldfish won at funfairs rarely survive?

A These poor goldfish are usually kept in far too cramped conditions, and in temperatures that change a lot very quickly. The best advice is to stay well away from this sort of stall so that it goes out of business, but if you do get one

of these goldfish (in a plastic bag, I expect) don't tip it straight into a tank at home where the water temperature may be very different – suspend the bag plus the goldfish in your tank for an hour or two until the temperatures have evened out.

Q My fish keep sort of gulping at the surface. I thought they were hungry but they don't seem interested in food.

A It sounds like there isn't enough oxygen in the water. Siphon some water off and add some fresh water (at the same temperature of course) and think about getting a bubbler. If this happens out in a pond, spray some fresh water over the surface with a hosepipe. (It may be that there are a lot of rotting leaves in the pond using up the oxygen, or simply that it's a very hot day.)

Q One of my goldfish has got white spots all over it. Should I separate it from my other fish?

A Yes, though I'm afraid white spot disease, as it's known, is very easily passed on and your other fish may already have it. Put the affected fish in a separate tank (remember to make sure the water is the same temperature) and ask your vet or pet shop for a special liquid to add to the water. Follow the same procedure for a similar illness called white fungus disease.

Q Is it normal for goldfish to swim around for hours with a long trail of their mess hanging off them?

A No. This is a sign that your goldfish have constipation. Are you feeding them only on dry fish food? If so, try giving them a little green food like chopped lettuce every few days. You could also try gradually raising the temperature of the water by a few degrees.

Q I've got some sticklebacks but they keep attacking each other.

A You'll find it's the males who are fighting. They are the ones with the red bellies and you should only have one in a tank (with as many females as you like, provided the tank is not overcrowded). Males will even attack a plasticine model wiggled about in the tank if it has a red belly!

Cats are just about the most beautiful, graceful and strokeable creatures in the whole of the animal kingdom. They are also very independent – unlike dogs they go out for long periods on their own, they often ignore you when you call them, and generally they do a very good impression of not needing you at all. Don't be fooled by this! Taking on a cute, cuddly kitten means caring for it every day for the next twelve to fifteen years.

Should you get a cat if you live in a flat? Well, some people think it's cruel if cats can't get out, but I'm not so sure. So long as you have some toys and a good litter tray that you clean out every day, I'd rather see a cat running around in a flat than joining the many abandoned cats on the streets (thousands of which get run over each year).

Home
Wash the blanket or cushion regularly to get rid of fleas and their eggs.

Scrub the basket as well to get rid of any flea eggs.

Handling
Support the cat underneath – don't let its hind legs swing free when you are carrying it. As with all animals hold firmly but gently. If you are going to take the cat in a car, put it in a secure wicker travelling basket or a cardboard RSPCA pet carrier. Loose cats in cars are dangerous.

What do I need?

A cat flap . . . will give me much greater freedom to come and go as I please.

Vaccinations . . . for fatal illnesses like cat flu at about two months old, and then booster injections every year. At the same time I may well need some powder or sprays for fleas.

Water   I don't drink much, but always leave some fresh water out for me. Once I'm grown up I really don't need milk, particularly if I'm a little overweight.

A collar and name disc   The collar is usually a special one to help prevent fleas, but the most important thing is that it's elasticated so I can slip it off if I get caught on anything.

A litter tray   If I'm kept in overnight this is essential! Please clean it out every day.

Home . . . is a basket or old chair tucked away in a quiet place in the house. Although it's tempting for both of us, *don't* let me share your bed – or we'll probably end up sharing it with fleas as well!

Food   Tinned food will leave me very contented, especially if you vary them a bit – don't let me get hooked on one particular dish like liver or something. Feed me twice a day as directed on the tin. Kittens will need smaller quantities more often.

FASCINATING ▶ FACTS FILE

Cats that like to swim

All cats are able to swim, though they will avoid water if they possibly can – apart from the Turkish Van cat. This pretty cat – white with an orange tail – really enjoys taking a dip. Maybe it's a distant cousin of the tiger, which loves to relax and play in the water.

Not just a beautiful body

A cat's whiskers help it to judge whether it can get through a small gap – the whiskers are almost exactly the same width as its body and are extremely sensitive.

A cat's rough tongue helps it to pull fur out when grooming, and is also useful when lapping up milk or water.

A cat's tail has many uses: to help balance when jumping, to warn enemies to stay away, to keep flies away, and even to keep draughts out when the cat's curled up.

Cat naps

The average cat sleeps for a total of about sixteen hours in each twenty-four hour day. So if a cat lives to be fifteen years old it will have slept away around ten of those years.

Olympic champions

The cheetah is the fastest land animal in the world, reaching around 110 km/hr (70 mph) as it goes for a kill. But it can only keep up this speed for a short sprint, so even much slower animals can escape if they are not caught by the cheetah within about ten seconds.

That's just purr-fect

Cats are the only members of the animal kingdom that are able to purr. They make this continuous noise by vibrating bits of their insides while taking each breath. Purring usually means 'That's great, please carry on!', though very occasionally it can be a sign that a cat is really unhappy. It's not only domestic cats that do it: all the smaller wild cats like lynx and bobcats also purr.

Dear Terry

Q Every now and then my cat has a loud coughing fit where she seems to be sort of clearing her throat and going 'ick, ick, ick'. Then she is usually sick.

A This is almost certainly nothing to be alarmed about. Your cat is probably clearing out hair that she's swallowed when grooming herself. She may well eat grass to help her throw up, so if you live in a flat with no garden keep a plant-pot of grass specially for the cat.

Q I saw my cat in the garden playing with a bird and then killing it. How can I stop him doing this?

A You can't! Cats are hunters by instinct. They go for small animals like birds and mice and their method of attack is with their claws. Feeding your cat more won't help: well-fed cats make the best 'mousers'! A name disc or even a small bell on an elasticated collar will make a noise and give the bird a chance to escape when your cat pounces.

Q Is there any way I can keep my cat out of fights? He's always coming back with a badly scratched face.

A I suspect you may not have had him neutered, and I would guess also that your house may be a bit smelly – a tomcat likes to spray urine over his territory. Neutering will stop this habit and should stop him getting into quite so many fights, though you might also think about keeping him in at night. Generally I think that all cats, male and female, should be neutered at about six months old, as there are already so many millions of unwanted kittens in the world.

Q When we go on holiday for a few weeks, should we take our cat with us or leave it at home?

A A neighbour who is prepared to come in twice a day and feed your cat at home is probably the best answer, though if you can afford it a good local cattery is also a safe bet.

Q I've noticed that our cat has bald patches in her fur. What causes these?

A This could be a variety of problems. It may be that flea bites have caused sores, or it may be a kind of fungus called ringworm. Since ringworm can be passed on to humans, especially children, avoid contact with the cat and get it to a vet immediately. (Wrap a towel around the cat before picking it up. This is also a good tip if a cat is injured or frightened.)

Q We've already got a cat and we're thinking of getting a dog. Will the cat mind?

A It might be a little upset for a day or two, but then the two animals will probably get on really well. Keep making a fuss of your cat to show it's still loved when the dog first arrives, but don't keep taking the dog away – the cat must get used to the idea that it's around for good.

Rats and mice

Pet rats and mice have had very bad publicity over the years because of their wild relatives (who destroy huge amounts of the world's food and can cause terrible diseases – see the Fascinating Facts File overleaf). But of course the rats and mice you buy in a pet shop have been specially bred, and probably carry less risk of disease than the average pet dog.

They are as easy to keep as gerbils and hamsters and are usually even more tame and friendly – they become real characters and will often perform little party tricks for you.

The only disadvantages are that their homes can smell a bit more musty than those of other small rodents, and also that friends (or parents) can be rather frightened of them until they discover what smashing little creatures they are!

Rats tend to be far bigger than mice and so need much larger cages or tanks. On average, mice live to the age of two or three and rats live about a year longer.

Home

Two mice should have a space at least 40 cm long, 30 cm wide and 30 cm tall (1½ ft by 1 ft by 1 ft), and a pair of rats will need 100 cm by 50 cm by 30 cm (3½ ft by 1½ ft by 1 ft).

Sawdust or peat with strips of white paper or straw for bedding

Handling

Mice can be picked up by the tail the same way as gerbils (see p. 10). A rat is usually too big to be picked up like this and needs supporting underneath. Like gerbils and hamsters, rats and mice may bite you if they get very frightened. As ever, be calm and gentle but confident too.

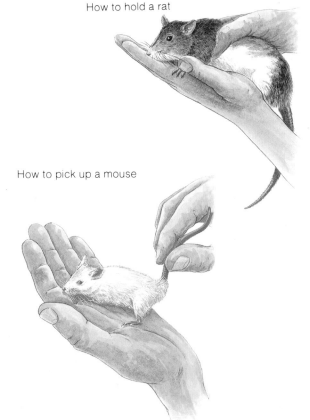

How to hold a rat

How to pick up a mouse

What do I need?

Cleaning out   Change my bedding every couple of days to prevent my tank or cage getting too smelly. Do a major cleaning job with hot water and special mild disinfectant about every three weeks (rinse thoroughly of course). Please do a daily clean out of rotten food.

A nice warm room . . . kept at about the temperature a human would like. Don't let my home get direct sunlight.

Company   I can live alone if you give me lots of attention, but really I also like another rat as a friend. Make sure we're of the same sex if you don't want us to breed. (The same goes for mice, who very much like to live in a group).

Water   Please change the water every day, and serve it in a drip-feed bottle.

Home . . . needs to be much bigger than you might think, and it's nice if it has several floors as I like to run up and down stairs. My bedroom is a small, dark box in a corner.

Food   The pellet or hamster mixes which you get from pet shops will do nicely – plus a little fruit and vegetables. Go easy on the cheese or you'll find I get rather smelly! Please don't let me become fat and lazy – feed me only about five level tablespoonfuls (about 30 g) of my pellets each day, and less if you're giving me lots of other things too. (The average mouse needs only one level tablespoonful.)

Toys   I like lots of interesting things to play with, like ladders, ramps and ropes to climb up, pipes or plant pots to crawl through, bark-covered twigs to gnaw at and a solid exercise wheel. (Please avoid cheap metal wheels with thin bars as I can hurt my paws or damage my tail on them.)

Mice or rats?
There is no real difference between mice and rats, though mice are usually smaller. The smallest of all is the Pygmy mouse with a body length of only 4½ cm (under 2 in) and a tail length of 3 cm (just over 1 in). The giant of the rat world is the Cuming's cloud rat with a body length of over 40 cm (nearly 1½ ft) and a tail of almost the same length.

Deep sleep

Many small animals hibernate in winter – their body cools, their heart slows down and they fall into a deep sleep for several months until the weather gets warmer and there is once again food to eat. The dormouse is one of the longest sleepers of all, hibernating for up to six months every year.

Complete pests

Rats and mice eat or destroy up to a third of the world's food, especially grain, rice and sugar. Huge armies of the animals burrow into food stores causing great damage to the buildings, and then the food they don't actually eat is spoiled by their droppings or their urine.

You dirty rat!

Wild rats spread many diseases – some are passed on in their droppings and their urine, while others can be caught by being bitten by an infected rat. The most devastating disease caused by rats is bubonic plague or Black Death. In just four years between 1347 and 1351 the plague killed millions of people across Europe, wiping out about a third of the population. It's only in the last hundred years that scientists have finally discovered a cure – and also discovered that the plague is passed on to humans by a flea living on the rat.

Dear Terry

Q I would like to buy some mice and start breeding them, and I'd like to know how long it takes before they have babies.

A Mice breed extremely quickly (rather like rabbits!). They start having babies when they are two or three months old, and pregnancy lasts for only three weeks. Since there can be up to twenty babies at a time, and since the mother can be pregnant again practically the same day, you'll get some idea of the huge number of mice you could very soon have around. You should think very carefully about whether you can find a good home for all these mice – the answer may be to separate the male mouse permanently from the female before she gives birth so that she only has one litter. That way you'll enjoy the wonders of it all – the nest building, the birth itself, the tiny babies which will fit inside a thimble! – without being completely overrun. But remember to separate the young male and female mice before they're about five weeks old, otherwise they will start having babies themselves!

Q Can you give me some advice about how to choose a rat that hasn't got any diseases?

A Rats are no different from any other pets bred in captivity – if you buy them from a good pet shop or breeder they should be disease-free. However, to make sure you get a really lively and healthy pet always go for the nosy animal with bags of energy which pushes to the front of the litter to get a better look at you. You should also check out the following: ears – clean with no cheesy or scabby stuff in them; eyes and nose – no 'gunk' and not runny; front paws – not wet or discoloured from nose-wiping; bottom – nice and clean; coat – sleek and smooth with no thin or bald areas.

Q All my mice seem to have colds – they are wheezing as they breathe, and have runny eyes and noses. Should I bother to take them to the vet's?

A Definitely, and as quickly as possible. Colds and chest problems are often far more serious in small animals than in humans. Mice and rats usually catch colds by being kept in damp, draughty cages. Some colds can be cured if treated quickly enough, but unfortunately others turn into a type of pneumonia and can't be treated.

Q My rat seemed fine when I bought it, but as soon as I got it home it got diarrhoea. Should I take it back to the shop?

A It's probably not necessary. An upset stomach is quite common in the first few days of a new pet coming home. It's usually caused by giving the animal food that it's not used to, but if the diarrhoea hasn't cleared up in a day or so take your rat to the vet. As a general rule, always ask the pet shop or breeder what food the animal has been getting, and then gradually change if you need to.

Frogs and toads

Frogs and toads are amphibians, which means they spend a lot of time both on land and in water. People often imagine that they are 'slimy and horrible', but in reality they are quite beautiful (yes, even before they are kissed by the beautiful princess!).

They make fascinating pets, none more so than the increasingly popular fire-bellied toad. This stunning, tiny creature grows to only about 5 cm (2 in) at most, with the male rather smaller than the female. It has a dark back with black speckles, and a red or yellow belly. When threatened it will stand on its hind legs and show off its bright belly to try to frighten away its enemy. If this doesn't work it may well hold its paws over its eyes as if this will make the enemy go away!

Fire-bellies and other amphibians bred in captivity can be bought reasonably cheaply from good pet shops and may live for around seven or eight years. I wouldn't recommend taking frogs and toads from the wild – apart from the possibility of disease it is often against the law for conservation reasons.

Tank

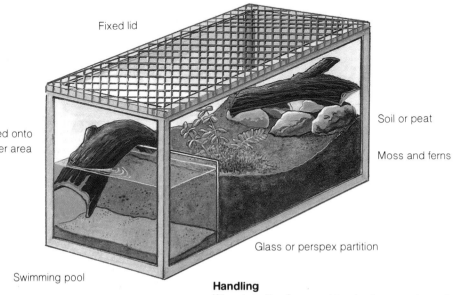

Fixed lid

Cork bark wedged onto one half of water area

Soil or peat

Moss and ferns

Glass or perspex partition

Swimming pool

Handling
When handling frogs and toads always wet your hands first and don't hold too tightly. Hold them over their tank or a table – they like to jump.

What do I need?

Food . . . twice a week only. I like live worms, slugs, woodlice, spiders: anything that moves that I can get in my mouth.

Company I like sharing the tank with a companion, but if we're of the opposite sex there is a small chance we'll breed.

Water . . . to keep my cage damp. A plant spray used every two or three days should do the trick.

Home . . . is a big damp tank with plenty of plants. It must have a good fixed lid with a fine mesh, otherwise I'll climb up the glass and escape!

A light place to live . . . if possible near a window-sill, but the tank must only get a few hours of either morning or late afternoon sun.

A 'swimming pool' Either partition off a section of the tank, or use a large plastic bowl or ice-cream container instead. Please change the water every two or three weeks using water which has stood in the same room overnight.

Cleaning out Dead food should be removed after a few hours, and the water changed every few days. Give the tank a thorough cleaning every month or two using a mild disinfectant (but please rinse the tank very thoroughly).

Flying frogs
In the jungles of South East Asia lives a frog which glides from tree to tree. Its huge webbed feet act like parachutes when the flying frog stretches out its arms and legs.

Amazing amphibians

Amphibians like frogs and toads lay eggs (called spawn) in water. When the eggs hatch the resulting tadpoles breathe through gills like fish and can only live underwater. But over the next few months remarkable changes begin to take place: legs start to develop, the gills and tail disappear, and the tadpole becomes a small frog or toad which comes out of the water and breathes air using lungs.

The most poisonous animal in the world

The tiny and colourful arrow-poison frog has a poison so strong in its skin that a small drop will instantly kill a large animal like a leopard. The frog's bright orange stripes warn enemies not to try to eat it. The name of the arrow-poison frog comes from the fact that its poison is used by South American Indians on the tips of their arrows.

Long-jump champions

Frogs are famous for being the world's great long-jumpers. The champion is a type of African frog which can leap forty-five times its own length. But nature's high-jump champion is the humble flea, which manages 130 times its own height.

Swallow that!

Most animals use their tongues to help them swallow (try swallowing hard and see for yourself). But the tongues of frogs and toads are fastened down at the front of their mouths, so instead they push food down with the backs of their eyes.

Dear Terry

Q Is it all right to collect frogspawn?

A Yes – so long as you eventually release the young frogs back into the wild you will be helping conservation by making sure some types of frog don't die out completely. Take only a little spawn, and take some pond water with it. Add some plants when you get home as the baby tadpoles will feed on them. As the tadpoles get bigger give them a little of the 'flaky' sort of fish-food (but clear it out of the water after a few hours if they don't eat it). As soon as they turn into little frogs and begin to crawl about, they are ready to go back to their pond. If you want to keep them for a little while longer, remember that they will now need live food just like adult frogs and toads – but don't leave it too late in summer

before returning them to the wild as they won't have time to build themselves up to survive their winter hibernation.

Q I've just got two fire-bellied toads, but as I was putting them in the tank I noticed they were covered in a sort of white froth which made my eyes water. What's wrong with them?

A Nothing at all! When they are frightened fire-bellies give off a white poison fluid through their skin. It's a little unpleasant and sometimes makes you sneeze, but it is not harmful to humans. Treat your toads gently and they should soon get used to you and stop doing this. Do remember to moisten your hands before you handle them and of course wash your hands afterwards.

Q I always thought frogs and toads caught their food by flicking out their tongue, but my fire-bellies never do this. Instead they just sort of snap at worms and spiders, and then gobble them up bit by bit. Is there something wrong with their tongues?

A No, but full marks for observation. You're absolutely right that most frogs and toads do flick out their tongues to catch their prey – the tongue is fastened down at the front of the mouth rather than the back so that it can be whipped out really quickly, and it's covered in a gooey substance so that the victim sticks to it. However, the fire-bellied toad is an exception – its tongue is fixed to the bottom of the mouth all the way along so it can't be flicked out.

Q I think one of my toads hurt herself on a stone, but she doesn't seem to be getting any better – the 'graze' just seems to have got worse.

A As a general point, always check carefully that stones or other objects you put in a cage or tank haven't got any sharp bits. I suspect in this case that your toad's wound has got infected by a type of fungus. This is quite common and your vet will probably 'paint' on some special liquid to clear it up.

Rabbits and guinea pigs

Rabbits and guinea pigs make excellent pets. But which to choose? Well, rabbits always seem to me to be a bit livelier and to have a bit more personality, but on the other hand guinea pigs are usually a little smaller and easier to pick up – they will rarely struggle or scratch. Rabbits need a larger hutch than guinea pigs, but are tougher and won't need the hutch brought indoors as often. One interesting difference is that guinea pigs have a strange, high-pitched squealing cry, whereas rabbits are usually silent (apart from their habit of thumping the ground with their hind legs to warn other rabbits that danger is near).

Rabbits come in all sizes and I would recommend that you go for a small to medium breed, as children will find it difficult to pick up one of the large breeds (which can grow to about 7 kg/ 15 lb). Rabbits live for about six or seven years – a year or two longer than the average guinea pig.

Hutch

Drip-feed water bottle

Sloping roof, weatherproofed to keep out damp

Hay rack fixed to back of hutch.

Wire mesh covering 'living-room'

Litter of wood shavings or moss-peat on newspaper or removable shelf

The smallest hutch for one guinea pig should be at least 60 cm (2 ft) long, 45 cm (1½ ft) wide and 30 cm (1 ft) tall. One medium-sized rabbit will need a hutch almost twice as big as this. The hutch will need to be put in a shed during really cold weather (but not in a garage with car fumes).

'Bedroom' with well-fitting door

Litter, as in 'living-room', but with lots of straw on top

Hutch should be raised about 30 cm (1 ft) off the ground to keep damp and other animals out.

Handling

Always support rabbits and guinea pigs underneath, and never pick up a rabbit by its ears. Try to get rabbits used to being handled from an early age, otherwise they can kick out with their hind legs and scratch you.

Home . . . is outside in a large dry wooden hutch raised off the ground. It should have a cosy bedroom and an airy living-room.

Company I can get very bored if I'm kept on my own. Two or three does (females) together is best, as bucks (males) always end up fighting (and a mixture of does and bucks will end up 'breeding like rabbits'!). You can keep either male or female guinea pigs together if they've known each other from an early age.

What do I need?

Cleaning out Soiled litter, droppings and uneaten food should be removed every day, and food bowls washed. Every few weeks the whole hutch needs a good scrub.

Clean, fresh water To prevent me from spilling it everywhere, use one of those drip-feed bottles with a tube. Change my water every day.

Food My breakfast is a bit like yours – a cupful of my own special rabbit cereal mix. Supper is fresh vegetables. (Note: not just lettuce and carrots, please!) I like to chomp away at hay all day, and I also like a bit of apple or pear as a treat. (Guinea pigs prefer two smaller meals of their own special cereal each day, plus lots of fruit and green vegetables.)

Exercise and grazing Keeping me in a hutch all day is like being in prison. Ideally my hutch should open out onto a grassy exercise area where I can run free and graze, but remember that I really will be free unless the area is fenced in both above and below ground!

Mad as a March hare

This old saying comes from the fact that the breeding season for hares usually starts around March, and at this time the male hare starts behaving very strangely: he will often get up on his hind legs and box with his front legs, and he scampers around pulling the fur out of the other males and kicking them with his hind legs.

The world's largest rodent

This is the capybara, which lives in South America and looks like a monster of a guinea pig. Capybaras are about the same size as a farmyard pig and are often eaten, so you could end up with capybara and eggs for breakfast!

Breeding like rabbits

Rabbits are famous for breeding quickly. Pregnancy lasts for around a month and a rabbit usually has between five and ten babies at a time. Some rabbits get pregnant ten times a year, producing a total of up to a hundred youngsters. These youngsters are themselves able to breed when they are just four months old.

Rabbits or hares?

The main difference is that rabbits live in groups in burrows, whereas hares usually live alone above ground. Hares can also usually run faster and further than rabbits.

Dear Terry

Q Why does my rabbit eat his droppings? Should I stop him doing this?

A *Well spotted! No, definitely don't stop him – this is an essential part of his diet! You may have noticed that he doesn't eat his main hard droppings, only smaller, softer ones. These are actually made up of food that the rabbit wasn't able to digest completely 'first time through'.*

Q My rabbits keep scratching their ears and seem to shake their heads more than they used to, as if they've got something in their ears.

A *You're right! They've almost certainly got ear mites, and if you look in their ears you may well see brown crusty bits caused by the mites. This is called ear canker and your vet should be able to clear it up quickly using special ear drops.*

Q My brother accidentally dropped my guinea pig a few centimetres onto the table. I think it's all right except that one of its front teeth broke off. Should I take it to the vet?

A *I don't think you'll need to in this case, but always be extra careful not to drop rabbits and guinea pigs, as they can get very bad spine injuries. As for the tooth, because guinea pigs are rodents their teeth keep growing throughout their life: within a couple of weeks your guinea pig should have a perfect new tooth! In the meantime, check that it hasn't got any bits of broken tooth in its mouth, and grate up any vegetables so that it can still eat them.*
Note by the way that rabbits' and guinea pigs' teeth can sometimes grow too long, and this obviously stops them eating properly. If this happens, your vet will clip the teeth – it sounds strange but it's really just like you or me cutting our nails.

Q My guinea pig seems to have lost weight and doesn't seem very well, and she dribbles a lot from her mouth.

A *It's possible that one of her teeth has got too long, stopping her eating (see the earlier question about teeth), but it's more likely that she's not getting enough vitamin C.*

Guinea pigs must have vitamin C every day and they get it from fresh fruit and vegetables. You should also put a vitamin C tablet in her water until she's well again (dissolve a fresh tablet in the water every time you change it).

Q Can I cut my guinea pig's nails, or should I let the vet do this?

A *Unlike teeth, which are always a job for the vet, you can cut back any rodent's claws yourself once you know how. Ask your vet to show you how it's done – the main thing is to avoid cutting into the darker bit of the nail which will bleed badly and hurt your pet like crazy.*

Notes on other pets

BUTTERFLIES

NOT RECOMMENDED

These beautiful, delicate creatures start life rather less attractively as caterpillars. Once they become butterflies they usually don't live very long – a few days or at most a few months. To keep them in captivity you need a special greenhouse with an enclosed porch (so they can't escape when you go in or out).

SNAILS

Snails are easy to keep and great fun to handle! Home is an old aquarium with gravel, soil and bark in the bottom. Keep the tank moist with a plant spray, and make sure it has a tight-fitting lid (otherwise the snails will 'zoom' off!). Feed on lettuce, potatoes and fruit.

LIZARDS

There are lots of different types of lizard with lots of different needs. In general they like similar conditions to snakes – for example a warm area of the tank to 'sunbathe' in plus some live food, but check up on the lizard's requirements before you buy it.

OTTERS

NOT RECOMMENDED

One of my first jobs as a boy was looking after otters. We had some great adventures but they really were a full-time occupation. Otters in the house cause complete chaos, finding their way inside everything from pillows to sofas! For the last ten years or so, otters have been a protected species.

BIRDS OF PREY

NOT RECOMMENDED

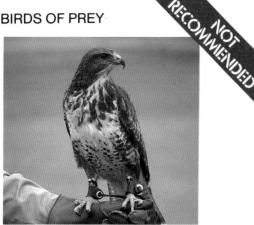

These include birds like eagles, buzzards and falcons which kill small animals for food. Their talons are sharp and powerful, and the birds must be treated with great care and respect. They need to fly outside every day, and handlers usually wear a leather glove. Training the bird to fly back and perch on their hand is definitely one for an expert!

TORTOISES

NOT RECOMMENDED

Tortoises are now a protected species (because of the danger that they will become extinct), and it is against the law to bring them into Britain. If you are offered one by a friend, please make sure before accepting that you know about its needs. For example, many people don't realise that tortoises must have a sheltered 'den' filled with straw to protect them from the cold at night.

STICK INSECTS

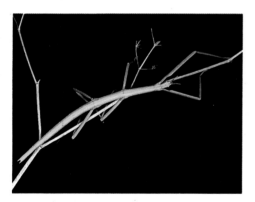

Stick insects really do look just like sticks, which is the perfect camouflage as they like to live in privet hedges. To keep them in captivity place several privet twigs inside a large well-ventilated cabinet or tank (the privet provides their food). Moisten the leaves every day with a plant spray, and replace the privet as soon as it begins to droop. But watch out – it's all too easy to throw out a stick insect as well by mistake!

TERRAPINS

NOT RECOMMENDED

Terrapins can be carriers of a disease called salmonella. They are also quite difficult to keep successfully, needing a warm tank of water heated to around 30°C, a constant supply of live food and a daily clean-out of left-overs from the water. If you do decide to keep them remember to provide a large dry area in the aquarium with a lamp above it so that the terrapins can 'sunbathe'.

Acknowledgements

Photographs

Front cover Bruce Coleman (top left, bottom right, Hans Reinhard; top right, M. Fogden); **page 8** Ardea (top, John Daniels), Bruce Coleman (left, Jane Burton; right, Hans Reinhard); **page 12** Bruce Coleman (top, Jane Burton; right, Hans Reinhard); **page 16** Bruce Coleman (top, Jen & Des Bartlett; left, Gordon Langsbury; centre right, Dieter & Mary Plage; bottom right, Bob & Clara Calhoun); **page 20** Zoological Society of London (right); **page 24** Bruce Coleman (left, John Visser; right, Hans Reinhard); **page 28** Bruce Coleman (top, Jane Burton; right, J. Fennell; left, Carl Roessler); **page 32** Sonia Halliday (top), Bruce Coleman (left, Jane Burton & Kim Taylor), Ardea (right, Y. Arthus-Bertrand); **page 36** Bruce Coleman (top, Jane Burton; left, Rocco Longo; top right, Andy Purcell), Mary Evans Picture Library (bottom right); **page 40** Ardea (top, Adrian Warren), Bruce Coleman (left, Rod Williams; right, Kim Taylor); **page 44** Bruce Coleman (top, Hans Reinhard; left, Mike Price; right, Gordon Langsbury); **page 46** Bruce Coleman (top left, G. Doré; bottom left, J. Andrada; bottom right, Gordon Langsbury); **page 47** Bruce Coleman (bottom left, Frieder Sauer; bottom right, M. Fogden).

Picture research: Jennifer Fry.

All the remaining photographs were taken at Windsor Safari Park for the BBC by David Gee.

Published by BBC Books, a division of BBC Enterprises Limited, Woodlands, 80 Wood Lane, London W12 0TT
First published 1989

© 1989 Terry Nutkins and Marshall Corwin/BBC Enterprises Limited

Paperback ISBN: 0 563 34524 1
Hardback ISBN: 0 563 34523 3

Printed in Great Britain by BPCC Paulton Books Limited
Typeset by Ace Filmsetting, England
Origination by Dot Gradations, England